C000259831

The Little Book of Small Dick Energy

First published in Great Britain in 2023 by

Greenfinch
An imprint of Quercus Editions Ltd
Carmelite House
50 Victoria Embankment
London EC4Y 0DZ

An Hachette UK company

Copyright © 2023 Quercus Editions Ltd

All rights reserved. No part of this publication may be reproduced or transmitted
in any form or by any means, electronic or mechanical, including photocopy,
recording, or any information storage and retrieval system, without permission
in writing from the publisher.

A CIP catalogue record for this book is available from the British Library

HB ISBN 978-1-52943-332-6
Ebook ISBN 978-1-52943-460-6

Quercus Editions Ltd hereby exclude all liability to the extent permitted by law
for any errors or omissions in this book and for any loss, damage or expense
(whether direct or indirect) suffered by a third party relying on any information
contained in this book.

10 9 8 7 6 5 4 3 2 1

Design by Luke Bird
Illustrations by Jo Parry
Printed and bound in Great Britain by Clays Ltd, Elcograf S.p.A.

Papers used by Greenfinch are from well-managed forests and other
responsible sources.

The Little Book of Small Dick Energy

Donald Tate

greenfinch

Introduction

Ever since the creation of dicks, there has been Small Dick Energy (SDE). The love child of low self-esteem and a need for approval, it has been repelling people from caves, pubs, offices and Formula 1 tracks since the dawn of time. Today, thanks to social media, no one is safe from having it waved in our faces willy-nilly.

Crucially, Small Dick Energy and its infinitely more pleasant cousin, Big, has nothing to do with anatomy. The energy we give off is abstract, invisible, infinite, with the potential to be more powerful and upsetting than any single dick could ever dream of. When left to fester unchallenged, Small Dick Energy can be responsible for failed relationships, ruinous business decisions, environmental destruction and even full-scale invasions of other countries. Even the most cursory look through mankind's most disastrous moments will reveal the same culprit at their centre without fail: the scared, desperate, sweaty monster that is Small Dick Energy.

With so much at stake, the need for a guide to this phenomenon is both self-evident and urgent. This by-no-means exhaustive list of SDE examples is here to help you spot the signs in someone who may be suffering from the affliction, whether they're your colleague, flatmate, teacher,

4

ex-boyfriend*, father or Deputy Prime Minister. With your trusty book in hand, you'll be able to identify the human trapped inside this layered complex and, once you've had a nice long cringe, offer your support.

Approach slowly, calmly, with no sudden movements and, if they haven't spooked, offer them a hug, a cup of tea, perhaps a copy of *Men's Health*. Quiet, positive affirmations will also help: 'You are enough, without having to rev up a supercar, blow cigar smoke in a passerby's face or loudly record a podcast about crypto inside a full Tube carriage.'

If you recognise any of these examples in yourself, don't panic. Instead of thinking with your (metaphorical) dick, use your brain to reflect on why you might be exhibiting these SDE traits. Is there an insecurity that lies at their heart? Remember, there isn't a single person out there who doesn't experience self-doubt; it's how we deal with these feelings that determines the size of our dick-energy. And, as the old saying goes, it's not the size of your dick-energy that matters, it's how you use it.

*This book focuses mainly on how SDE manifests in males but it is important to note that females aren't immune from the condition (nor its bigger counterpart), and there are plenty of examples which apply to both. SDE does not discriminate, which is partly what makes it so dangerous.

Examples of

Small
Dick
Energy

Not wearing
a jumper when
it's −2°C to
ensure everyone
can see their
'Tough Mudder:
Finisher' T-shirt.

Finding out someone at dinner is vegetarian, so ordering the steak and eating it in front of them, mouth-open, making loud pleasure-noises.

Owning a signed copy of
*The Game: How to
Pick Up Women.*

Refusing to use the shorter urinal in the service station bathroom.

Password is cryptolegend007.

Refers to 'Elon', like they're mates.

Uploading Instagram posts of their cigar humidor with the caption: 'Come to daddy.'

Not asking the person next to them at dinner a single question, showing them 200 pics of their trip to Vegas, then later accusing them of being 'boring' and 'not very talkative'.

Calling friends 'whipped' for doing things like attending their girlfriend's/ boyfriend's birthday dinner.

Turns off a film when they realise it's a musical.

Writes essays defending Clarkson in the comments section of MailOnline.

Loudly orders a vindaloo then, drowning in their own sweat, tells the waiter it's not hot enough.

Describes their salary as 'big boy money'.

Enforces uni drinking rules on their table at weddings.

Doesn't just bring a guitar to the party but brings an amp as well.

Proudly and repeatedly tells people they don't cry.

Leaves comments under porn videos criticising the technique of the actors.

Invades Ukraine.

Calls themselves
a 'boob man'
like it's their
Hogwarts house.

Panic-punches their friends hello because they're too emotionally inarticulate to hug. Always a little bit too hard.

LinkedIn job title: 'Professional Troublemaker'.

Photoshops their Spotify Wrapped to hide all the Olivia Rodriguez tracks.

Describes themselves as the 'alpha' of their badminton team.

Absolutely worships Ronaldo. Constantly describes him as 'the perfect specimen' then gets very defensive when asked if they fancy him.

Only ever shakes hands with and addresses the senior men in meetings.

Tries to mentor every young person they meet then, when they're rejected, says things like: 'There's absolutely no hope for that generation'.

Constantly tells people that they're 'absolutely brilliant' with mums, when it turns out they're just very flirty in a weirdly patronising way.

Never passes in five-a-side football. Always does endless stepovers, gets tackled, then blames their teammates for not being open.

Only listens to two podcasts: *The Joe Rogan Experience* and their own podcast, *The Lion's Roar*, which is mainly them blasting Disney remakes for being too 'woke'.

Yells 'Big dog alert!' when walking into any room, including empty ones.

Never lets their child win at anything.

Says therapy is for losers who can't cope with life, then punches a hole in their bedroom wall when they get killed in *Call of Duty*.

Gives themselves nicknames that heavily utilise 'the' and never catch on, e.g.
The Jaguar,
The Penetrator,
The King of the North.

Writes essays on LinkedIn telling people they're bound to be broke losers forever unless they start the day with an ice bath and a shot of bull sperm.

Only ever refers to drinking water as 'hydrating'.

Yells profanity-laden tactics from the sidelines at their kid's football match, then tells the coach they'll handle the half-time team talk because they once had a trial at West Ham. (It was a trial to be a waiter in the canteen.)

Puts one leg up on things, spreads their legs and very slowly thrusts their hips back and forth at the person they're talking to.

Quick to inform
any woman who
makes them
laugh that she's
'actually quite
funny, for a girl'.

Keeps a hyper-vigilant eye on everyone else's pints to make sure they're not the last to finish theirs, but also not the first to finish so they don't have to get the next round.

Calls anyone who doesn't laugh at their offensive jokes 'a snowflake', then storms off in a rage when told that they're not funny.

Frequently heard saying 'What's wrong with you? Forgot your tampons?' to any man who looks even mildly annoyed.

Stalks women around the gym offering to help with the equipment, saying, 'I just used the shoulder press so you're going to want to turn down the resistance, babe.'

Frequently calls friends 'a little bitch' for doing things like eating vegetables.

Vigorously maintains that the female orgasm is a myth.

Pays for a blue tick on Twitter.

Argues against literally any point made by anyone else, then says 'Sorry, I can't help it – I'm just more intellectually engaged than most people.'

Posts nonsensical quotes about business, sloppily photoshopped onto pictures of Tommy Shelby.

Shockingly firm handshake. Terrifyingly sweaty.

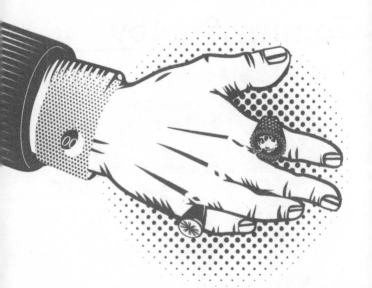

Will remind anyone at any point that people like them, Muhammad Ali and Jeff Bezos are 'built different'.

Has two burner Instagram accounts. One where they DM models and one where they abuse footballers.

Posts YouTube videos called things like 'Covid is a hoax – what the snowflakes don't want you to know' with the caption: 'Thank me later.'

Adding a spoiler, spinning rims and an undecipherable customised number plate to their Nissan Micra.

Often found
commenting
'King' under any
posts from toxic
male influencers.

Shrieks hysterical tears alone in bed every night.

Tweets Daisy
Ridley once a
week with,
'Your weekly
reminder that
you ruined
Star Wars.'

Pushes in front of children to get off the plane first.

Favourite joke is to explain what mansplaining is to a woman.

Waking up at 5am to do revenge press-ups because they lost at Monopoly the night before.

Claims women are only pretending to like football so they can gatecrash 'lads' time'.

Mistakes any member of the opposite sex showing them the tiniest modicum of politeness as a display of sexual desire.

Bowling name: The Kingpin. Also brings their own ball and if anyone else tries to use it, yells: 'Hey, that's the King's!'

Claims to know someone in literally every establishment. Talks to bouncers/barmen/mechanics like they've been friends for years, laughing hideously loudly at anything they say and looking round to see if anyone's noticing.

Likes to say,
'What is this,
a hen do?',
whenever anyone
on a stag drinks a
coffee or a glass
of water.

Pronouns:
he/hero.

Says things like: 'No offence but if these female "comedians" want to see what real comedy is then they ought to have a night out with my mate Gaz.' (Gaz yells *Inbetweeners* quotes at younger women trying to enjoy their night then collapses in his own piss.)

Upon hearing what someone does for a living, interrupts to tell them everything they know and think about that job.

Beats their naked chest with both fists when a new series of *The Grand Tour* is announced.

Says things like,
'I've got too much
testosterone for
just one girl, babe,
you knew that
going into the
relationship.'

Opens a beer with a bottle opener then secretly pops the cap back on, looks around the party to see who's watching and pretends to wrench it off with their teeth.

Constantly, **constantly** describes themselves as totally confident and secure.

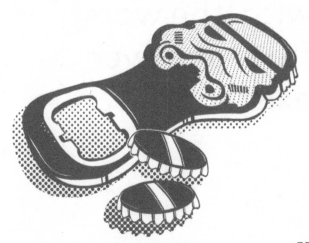

Repeatedly tells people that they never get ill, but won't hesitate to pull out of events moments before with 'the worst flu that's ever existed'.

Describes themselves as a 'thought leader' in their field.

Can't offer someone their seat on the tube without expecting the whole carriage to stand and applaud.

Has two modes
in a conversation:
broadcasting
and preparing to
broadcast.

Enjoys saying, 'If it weren't for all these oversensitive snowflakes, I'd be making a killing as a comedian.'

Most frequently
used emojis:
whisky glass,
raw meat,
crown, lion
and man lifting
weights.

Mocks the air steward during the safety briefing then watches *Entourage* out loud on their laptop without headphones.

Religiously observes and protects lads' night out every Saturday. Then, throws a hissy fit whenever their girlfriend is about to go out with her friends, collapsing into a heap at her feet and crying that 'no one likes him'.

Convinced that the entire world is against them whenever anything mildly inconvenient happens, like their train being delayed or their phone dying.

Refuses to acknowledge their very serious gluten allergy in case they appear weak.

Typical dating app opener: 'So how does someone as beautiful and innocent as you end up matching with a workaholic CEO and cigar connoisseur like me, eh? Oh well, best not to question it!'

Typical dating app follow-up: 'Going to give you the benefit of the doubt and assume you missed the above ^. Fortunately for you, chivalry isn't dead: I'm prepared to be patient, but most other men with my kind of schedule wouldn't be quite as polite ha ha.'

Outwardly self-identifies as an arsehole because it means less moral accountability and makes them feel cool. 'I don't know what to tell you – I'm an arsehole – I thought you knew that.'

Posts sincere, momentous captions like, 'Only the purest may flow through the veins of the most virtuous' on a selfie of them holding a green juice from Pret.

Dresses in full black tie and brings Thermos-martinis for the Bond premiere at the local Cineworld.

Likes posting pictures of random guys with long hair with the caption: 'Men, what happened? *sighs.'

Cheers when enemy soldiers are shot in war films.

Instagram Explore page is an orgy of fight videos, girls in bikinis and erectile dysfunction pills.

Bullies pets.

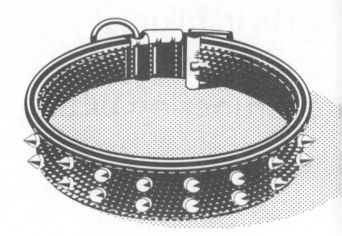

Google Search history:

Cool things to say
at party

How to speak
Jamaican patois

Cool accessories
for party

Hire bulldog

Buy bulldog fully grown

Can you give bulldog
away to dog's home
after one day?

Diamond collars

Signs off emails 'AG' (Always Grindin').